I0429353

DEDICATION

This book is dedicated to those working with The United Nations and Global Citizens that work daily paid and unpaid to help develop constructive policy leadership...

CONTENTS

"<u>LIBYA</u>"

My suggestion for the United Nations
"**Humanitarian Intervention**"
By
Harvey Carroll, Jr.
"<u>THE UNELECTED PRESIDENT</u>"

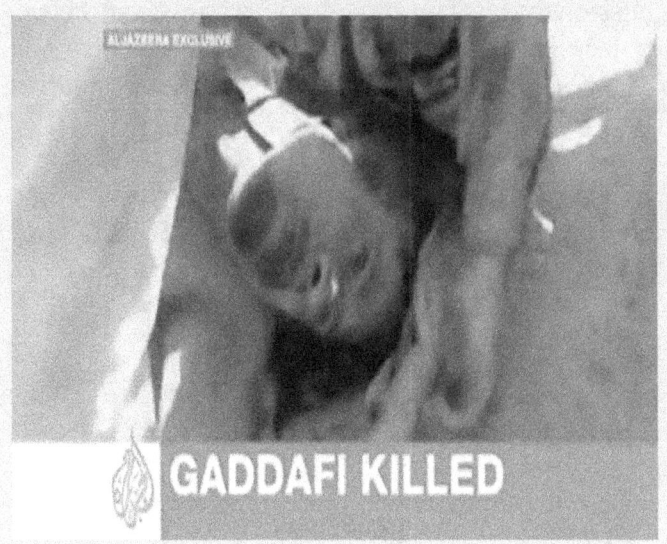

Copyright © 2016 Harvey Carroll, Jr.

All rights reserved. Including the right to reproduce my book, or portions thereof, in any form. No part of my text may be reproduced in any form without the express written permission of the author.

This is my book on Libya. I have written a near 30 page Poem on "Desert Storm." Books include a Mini-Autobiography "THE UNELECTED PRSIDENT), SCREWED, which is about the Lewinsky sex scandal and my involvement in Clinton's "Little White House Lie," and my "Operation Just Cause; "my suggestion for the Panama Invasion, my helping to organize and maintain the 1st Gulf War "Desert Storm" my missionary mission turned military mission; hence, "Black Hawk Down," and this book on Libya and my suggestions for U.N. "Humanitarian Intervention."

I intend to publish a series of Books under the trademark "THE UNELECTED PRESIDENT"

ISBN-13:

978-1530079230

ISBN-10:

1530079233

ACKNOWLEDGMENTS

I wish to thank my friends and family for being patient with me... I know I spend a great deal of time focusing on the World and less on them... I am sorry for that, but I have notices what happens to others often reflect how our own lives are better or worse... We should try to do better to get better...

1
MY SUGGESTIONS
FOR
UNITED NATIONS
"HUMANITARIAN
INTERVENTION"
INTO LIBYA

As Global Citizens we should strive to solve problems, as opposed to becoming part of the problem...

In my attempt to solve problems in Libya, resulted in becoming part of the problem in Syria...

Citizens and Diplomats alike should realize that the key is to focus on long-term constructive policy development and not go for the short-term political soundbites for TV...

We simply have to make it clear that problems in the World or the problems in our lives rarely get solved quickly.

We must focus our time and attention; therefore, we must realize that the same time and attention has to be focused on solving very big problems around the world and the need for the best and brightest to dedicate years of their lives to solve such problems...

Solving the problem requires Diplomats, Department of Commerce-- Professional Public Administrator armed with "Comprehensive Planning Templates" that encourage Civil Society/Global Citizens to participate in creating growth and development, while adding more quality of life.

This type of focus makes great improvements to Local, Regional, State, and International Business must look at Public Private Partnership's opportunities to maintain political and economic stability...

Diplomats, Department of Commerce and Professional Administrators armed with "Comprehensive Planning Templates" must work together to create long term planning.

Local, Regional, State, as well as National and International Business must look at ways to expand Public Private Partnership opportunities. Business is the driver of the real economy that maintains political and economic stability...

The Results will be far more affective in the long run...

Now I will give you an example of how both Libyan and Syrian policy making came about and why such care and attention must be used to develop constructive policy making...

Sadly, my constructive suggestions for "Humanitarian Intervention" into Libya went a bit extreme; as opposed to my "Divide Libya Policy" the U.S. Ambassador Stevens armed Benghazi and other Rebels (it got himself killed as I warned could happen via fb to his fellow Diplomat--Sr. Clinton/Obama Advisor).

U.S. President Obama and Secretary of State Clinton gave into the Hawks of Washington and began calling for Gadhafi regime change ultimately led to the Ambassador and fellow Diplomats death... Yet, this was not totally their fault as the Republicans would like to make people believe.

Granted Gadhafi returned to his old way of being a bad Dictator, whom was leading his military on a murderous massacre into Misrata, and headed towards Benghazi in the East, but there was a Diplomatic window of opportunity that may have been able to prevent this if regime change had not become the norm...

I truly believe a more constructive "Divide Libya" policy could have prevented Civil Conflict in Libya... Yet, rhetoric in America during the Political Presidential race set reason aside that focused on short term as opposed to long term constructive Policy Making...

This United Nations overkill, which not only destroyed Gadhafi's Army-also led to the brutal and inhumane killing of Gadhafi. This brutal international display of inhumane death of the dictator touched even the strongest hawk hearts and minds.

The Gadhafi killing allowing Putin and Medvedev of Russia to cite Libya as a failure, as did Republican hawks, which President Obama had caved into in favor of regime change... I had great concerns for "Regime Change" in Libya and strongly voiced this to international political think tanks such as "The Council on Foreign Relations (CFR)."

I noticed that Dr. Haass of the CFR echoed my concerns to the Senate Hearing chaired by then Senator Kerry. The talk of hasty "Regime Change" in Libya led to series of unreasonable outcomes; Syria is one of them...

I think that U.S. Secretary of State Clinton was somewhat between the Hawks and constructive policy makers. Yet, I think she was well aware that Gadhafi had a brutal history; thereby, giving our U.S. Ambassador to Libya a lot of leeway, which allowed him to work more closely with the Department of Defense military minds to Arm rebel's...

This leeway that Secretary of State Clinton placed the Ambassador Steven's fate into the hands of the Defense hawks that failed to protect him...

2
LETTERS AND FB POST TO THE U.S. AMBASSADOR TO THE UN

A letter to my UN Ambassador Facebook friend concerning my involvement in suggesting the "Humanitarian Intervention in Libya, more specifically my more reasonable "Divide Libya Policy" that would have saved tens of thousands of lives and prevented hundreds of thousands of War Immigrants....

The United States and the United Nations has to remember, with power and influence, there is also responsibility... From my experiences, which have cost a number of lives in trying to be constructive, I would like to Diplomats/Policy Makers a bit of advice to keep them serving the public for a long time in a constructive way; while keeping their soul clean...

There will come a time, perhaps just ones daily reflection that you will start to contemplate your decision making and once you get over one's own pride.

Policy Makers will begin to wonder "if" their decisions were based on reason and rational, or were it more of a competitive ball game where one side had to win at all cost...

Then the stress will set in if they were a part of that decision making process and/or if others had managed to have more influence, which turned a constructive policy into a destructive policy...

The U.S./UN and NATO did well in Libya and I won't lecture you on Libya for they acted quickly to provide "Humanitarian Intervention"; however, I did advocate a "Divide Libya" policy that could have saved tens of thousands of lives and hundreds of thousands of war immigrants... Now, I know the Hawks and the old regime changers won out on this, and you may not feel responsible for the outcomes; however, it still hurts me personally, as I see this as a loss for Diplomacy.

Sure, many are boasting and a few are out beating their chest in pride... Yet, I know with all my heart things could have been more constructive for all concerned and I worry about this attitude affecting humanity on many levels as violence silences the voices of reason…

I see much of the same type of policy in Syria and this concerns me… I have been trying to use my voice of reason and ask how Diplomatic Delegations to Syria can create a win-win situation there instead of a "Death Democracy" transition… Democracy is great, but "Death Democracy"; whereby, every few years a coup and/or overthrow of a regime is not Democracy; therefore,

I hope Diplomacy voices of reason can keep humanity from going down these bloody paths of "Death Democracy from being the norm...

3
AFRICAN UNION FAILURES

My friends/contacts in the African Union are saying that they may have a full support presentation at the United Nations that would bring nearly 1 billion people to the table in support of the United Nations mandate:

I hear that the AFRICAN UNION http://www.au.int/en/ or www.africa-union.org is planning a large United Nations Presentation to show support for the U.S./UN/NATO operations in Libya...

I also have heard that at the U.N. Presentation that African Union plans to compare Africa with the United States in many ways such as each Country like a State, and in each State, that there are many large, well-developed cities, and that it is not the National Geographic version presented on kids programs.

I hear that the African Union intends to create a vast trade and commerce Block with the United States, and ask to become a more favored trade nation within the WTO. They also wish to show support for the U.N. mandate in Northern Africa having a unified population of nearly 1 Billion people...

The African Union does not wish to send troops into the region; however, nearly every African country said that if "Boots were to be on the Ground" then it should be African boots, unless outsiders were invited in as they have in the past...

I look forward to hearing and seeing the African Union, presentation and their show of respect and support for President Obama, and the United Nations mandate to protect lives in their efforts to separate the violence in Libya...

First reply from the African Union: Yoweri Kaguta Museveni is the President of Uganda
http://afolabi-kola.blogspot.com/2011/03/let-libyans-solve-their-own-problems-by.html#comment-form

A few quick points about your letter... It was Global Investors that you talk bad about that invested money in Libya to help develop the Oil and the infrastructure such as roads...

My view is that Capitalism "business" is not a bad thing; Government has its role to play in society as does business in order to maintain an economy...

I should know, I was one of the first to offer help to bail out the collapsed Soviet Union... Government and Business "Capitalism", working together via public/private partnerships great growth and development can occur in every community, city, state, and country within the World...

Here is a "Comprehensive Planning" tool to help... Feel free to use it and don't feel like a "PUPPET" just because you have been given a gift from a Westerner.

I want to see an end to the violence in Libya. I propose a "Divide Libya" policy... The East would obviously elect rebels, and the West would obviously elect Gadhafi. So, let this happen… The center Oil City of Ras Lanuf could become a U.N./AU Green Zone with two Libyan Flags on it…

This would keep the Oil and Investments flowing, redevelopment of the region and a larger more ambitious focuses on growth, development and democracy… Perhaps expand the cities…

I hope that you take the time to look at the human cost, the vast economic investments that the Global Community has in Libya instead of a narrow view that you currently see…

4

LIBYA AS A FAILED STATE; DIPLOMACY, DEMOCRACY AND DEVELOPMENT

The U.N. should focus on Diplomacy, Development and Democracy and Human Rights... With this in mind it makes more sense for the U.N. to call for Congressional and Presidential Elections in Libya, and call for a stop to the violence and this will prevent the U.N. from entering the country via a Peace Force...

Unlike many other national and international policy issues that I worked on, I cannot take credit for the recent U.N. mandate against Libya... Granted I "may have" had a bit of urgency influence via my letters to various Government contacts, and to the U.S. Ambassador to the United Nations as she clicked the Facebook "Like" button ...

I saw "no direct buzz-bites" or what I like to refer to as "Silly Sh!t" that I like to have Presidents say to let me know that I was part of the speech writing, and/or policy making process... I have heard nothing about "Dividing Libya", and/or other key points that I wrote about, which I felt were key issues in separating the Western supported Gadhafi, from the Eastern support of the Revelators...

I think in the future this issue will be revisited, and my policy position papers will be given a closer look... I hope not, but I can assure you that forces will be amassed into the region, and a close eye kept of Libya for some time to come... The cease-fire meets short-term security issues for those opposing Gadhafi, however, the "War Crimes" issue may not go away. This in turn will back Gadhafi into a corner leaving him with no other option but to fight...

Unless the "War Crimes" issue is addressed with the "Dividing of Libya" and a true U.N. recognition of a "Civil War" that allows Gadhafi's popularity in the West to recognize a "Self-Defense" and "Civil Unrest", then he will have future problems with the international community...

Gadhafi has clearly has lost the Eastern part of Libya which justifies "Dividing of Libya"…

While, the U.N. has a "No boots on the ground" policy and the problem of "2 Bloody Libyan Flags" flying over the Center of the Country's Oil Port City of Ras Lanuf, who but the U.N. Peace keepers can keep that area a "Green Zone" and maintain a Co-Existence and economic enhancement via Technical AID/Comprehensive Planning, where citizens now have a voice in their City/State Government.

President Obama, Dr. Susan Rice our Ambassador to the United Nations has provided quick leadership, organized supportive deals and gained abstainments to get the U.N. mandate approved on a near "Multi-national Coalition level that I helped organize and maintain during the 1st Gulf War"…

This makes me proud of American leadership that is working hard to try and be a part of the International Community as opposed to the "Your either with us or against us attitude that the Bush Administration presented"… In the short-term it will save lives, but the work is not done and more complex issues will have to be addressed…

5
NEEDING A PAT ON THE BACK
A BIT OF SELF TALK

A few Silly Sh!t Examples: Bush, Sr. stating "Drug Indicted Dictator" referring to General Manuel Noriega, and naming the Panama Invasion "Operation Just Cause" as it was a just cause to prevent hardcore drugs from entering the United States...

"Comparing Saddam to Hitler, and mentioning that he used Chemical Weapons against his own people" and the Saddam would not be going against people with Sticks and Stones, that he would be facing ...bla, bla, bla... Hell, I even Invoked "MC Hammer" and influenced Bush, Sr. to say "Its Hammer Time" bringing in the reality of dropping the hammer (shoot) at Saddam...

I won't bore you with the dozens of pages of "Silly Sh!t" that I have used to watch President say, but I will tell you that a small town Irvine boy needed to put in those things into speeches to maintain focus and counter the "can't do" attitude that is so prevalent where I grew up.

I loved the circle of people that I had around me and still today call them friends. I recognize that live in a comfortable, but blissful world of their own creation that in many ways I admire… They have kept me grounded, but could have also keep grand national security strategies from being completed if I didn't have my own mind and/or if I had feel under their non-believer influence…

Still today I have many friends that don't believe that I have done anything and that is okay, they have their lives and I have mine and we can still call "Bullsh!t" on each other without getting too upset… Even with a few letters from Presidents, Governors, and Senators there is not enough supportive evidence to really support my claims…

I don't foresee Airforce One dropping me off at the Coal Wash Airport anytime soon either… I've flown into that airport and it is too small to land, perhaps Marine One at the Fair Grounds.. lol…

Heck, I'm yet to be invited to stay in the Lincoln bedroom or sit in the Oval Office Chair to see how that feels for a while since I have only done so in my mind…

I can't help but to think that most of my friends would obviously prefer the thoughts of an intern BJ as opposed to the thoughts of being a Constructive World Leader, but that is okay also.

In many ways, Clinton was like my friend and I felt his pain ;-), and stress. So, I took the time to write papers that helped overt a war with Iraq during his term and asked him via James Carville's office to tell a "Little White House Lie" and not admit to the BJ as the First Lady was in Eastern Europe/Central Asia on an important Diplomatic Mission that I had suggested…

Lol, as you can see dozens around me were saying that I am just a small town guy that couldn't have such influence, I needed to include "Silly Sh!t" statements to remind me that I was in fact influencing national and international policy. Policy that saved millions of lives, and affected the economic fate of nations...

6
DIVIDING LIBYA WOULD HAVE PREVENTED A FAILED STATE

I just thought of a great "Buzz-Bite/Sound Bite" for Dividing Libya":

"U.S. and Global Partners policy in Libya is like separating kids in a sand box. However, the problem is that Libya is a very huge sandbox. Therefore, to keep it simple we have to start with the a separating Libya along political divides along the coastal cities first, with the center separation point being at Ras Lanuf"

Without a clear "Entry and Exit Strategy" such as the Dividing of Libya, which I have written about many times NATO and partners will have major issues that the World does not need at this point and time...

I know in my heart that NATO and my President Obama are having trouble defining a clear plan for Libya... Perhaps this will help a bit... I think everyone in the

World knows that the U.S. and the E.U. Countries along with our strategic allies in the World are the primary investors within the Libyan Oil Rich region...

Those large international corporations, Global pension funds, and mom and pop retirement funds have invested in the region to create a Global Gas Station... American only import 66,000 barrels @ about $100 a barrel from Libya it show that Libya; therefore, Libya is not America's primary gas station; however, it is home to many major investments that millions of American rely on for stable investments...

With the business aspects out of the way, we have to look at the toll that it is taking on the Libyan people and those that are trying to help them...

Millions of Libyan's along with many investors and Global workers that have business interest in Libya are fleeing the violence, being beaten, tortured, raped and slaughtered along the way... The continued violence adds to the Humanitarian problem that is "IF" there is not a U.N. Split then that humanitarian problem will become unmanageable... Especially, with the recent devastation from the Tsunami in Japan...

If Libya is NOT "Divided" I think that there will be millions of lives lost; therefore, a clear "DIVIDE" must occur, and I think this map helps show that "Libya is already Divided" http://www.bbc.co.uk/news/world-africa-12572593 So, the U.N./U.S./NATO and the World would only be separating the violence and protecting the Oil Rich City of Ras Lanuf

A nice interview on BBC's Hard Talk http://news.bbc.co.uk/2/hi/programmes/hardtalk/9436093.stm : I support and propose a "Divide Libya" policy to separate the East (Rebels) from the West (Gadhafi)... This will save millions of lives... I like you feel that Gadhafi and Diplomatic Discussions will be the final solution...

I strongly believe that the UN and NATO should have considered a "UN mandated Divide of Libya" If not, I am afraid that Civil Conflict and failed state will appear in Libya…

NATO should have just kept it simple and separate the bad kids in the sand box in Libya,…

7
ARAB LEAGUE

President Obama and NATO along with the Arab League need to show leadership. People in the World are having a difficult time due to the Global Economic Crises; people are losing jobs, homes, cars, and families due to economic hard times...

While we share concerns for the folks that want Democracy in "Part of Libya" Gadhafi is still popular and would be elected in the Western part of the Country... This has to be realized; therefore, the most reasonable answer is to "Divide the Country" and prevent Civil War...

All we had to do is... Keep it simple, this is the best "Entry and Exit Strategy", which keeps the conflict manageable, and gets it done quickly, while President Obama and other World Leaders can go back to Domestic politics, and the economy, to meet Global Citizen's needs...

Those of you that are good friends with President Obama, the NATO and other

Global Leaders, please take the time to share this with them… My credentials are strong and we need a win-win situation for all involved and to save millions of lives, prevent vast humanities issues…

I would put my credentials up against anyone that questioned this policy… I have vast success in analyzing and presenting position papers on conflicts in Panama, Somalia, 1st Gulf War planning and organizing the multi-national coalition, and I was a voice against returning to Iraq for the obvious reasons we see today.

I shared many thoughts on how to assist in Westernizing Eastern European policy after the collapse and much more... I consider myself pretty darn good at this stuff, and have saved millions of lives and affected the economic fate of nations to prove it… This is a real cry out and call for constructive leadership to focus on "Comprehensive Planning" Libya…

8
GADHAFI MAKES THREATES, HIS SON GIVES "DEATH AUTHORIZATION"

A vague inference by Gadhafi's son Saddi Gadhafi gave a vague authorization for the Benghazi Police to fire on the Peaceful Protesters. This is what started the Civil War…

This created the Divide and Gadhafi lost East Libya because of it… The Gadhafi's have no one to blame but themselves. I think that eventually, people would see that the Police panicked and fired on the protesters by exceeding the authorization. However, the incident created a clear "Divide" in Libya…

Without a clear "Entry and Exit Strategy" such as the Dividing of Libya, which I have written about many times NATO and partners will have major issues that the World does not need at this point and time…

I know in my heart that NATO and my President Obama are having trouble defining a clear plan for Libya... Perhaps this will help a bit... I think everyone in the World knows that the U.S. and the E.U. Countries along with our strategic allies in the World are the primary investors within the Libyan Oil Rich region...

Those large international corporations, Global pension funds, and mom and pop retirement funds have invested in the region to create a Global Gas Station... American only imports 66,000 barrels @ about $100 a barrel from Libya it show that Libya; therefore, Libya is not America's primary gas station; however, it is home to many major investments that millions of American rely on for stable investments...

With the business aspects out of the way, we have to look at the toll that it is taking on the Libyan people and those that are trying to help them...

Millions of Libyan's along with many investors and Global workers that have business interest in Libya are fleeing the violence, being beaten, tortured, raped and slaughtered along the way... The continued violence adds to the Humanitarian problem that is "IF" there is not a U.N. Split then that humanitarian problem will become unmanageable... Especially, with the recent devastation from the Tsunami in Japan...

If Libya is NOT "Divided" I think that there will be millions of lives lost; therefore, a clear "DIVIDE" must occur, and I think this map helps show that "Libya is already Divided" http://www.bbc.co.uk/news/world-africa-12572593 *So, the U.N./U.S./NATO and the World would only be separating the violence and protecting the Oil Rich City of Ras Lanuf*

I strongly believe that the UN and NATO should consider a "A UN mandated Divide of Libya" If not, I am afraid that millions could die and this become a long term conflict... NATO should just keep it simple and separate the bad kids in the sand box in Libya,...

President Obama and NATO along with the Arab League need to show leadership. People in the World are having a difficult time due to the Global Economic Crises; people are losing jobs, homes, cars, and families due to economic hard times... While we share concerns for the folks that want Democracy in "Part of Libya" Gadhafi is still popular and would be elected in the Western part of the Country... This has to be realized; therefore, the most reasonable answer is to "Divide the Country"... Keep it simple, this is the best "Entry and Exit Strategy", which keeps the conflict manageable, and gets it done quickly, while President Obama and other World Leaders can go back to Domestic politics, and the economy, to meet Global Citizens needs...

Those of you that are good friends with President Obama, the NATO and other Global Leaders, please take the time to share this with them... My credentials are strong and we need a win-win situation for all involved and to save millions of lives, prevent vast humanities issues…

I would put my credentials up against anyone that questioned this policy… I have vast success in analyzing and presenting position papers on conflicts in Panama, Somalia, 1st Gulf War planning and organizing the multi-national coalition, and I was a voice against returning to Iraq for the obvious reasons we see today.

I shared many thoughts on how to assist in Westernizing Eastern European policy after the collapse and much more... I consider myself pretty darn good at this stuff, and have saved millions of lives and affected the economic fate of nations to prove it… So, I understand clear and sensible policy making at the Presidential/UN/Global response level…

Remember, a vague inference by Gadhafi's son Saddi Gadhafi gave a vague authorization for the Benghazi Police to fire on the Peaceful Protesters. This is what started the Civil War... This created the

Divide and Gadhafi lost East Libya because of it...

The Gadhafi's have no one to blame but themselves. I think that eventually, people would see that the Police panicked and fired on the protesters by exceeding the authorization. However, the incident created a clear "Divide" in Libya...

9
13 HOURS-SECRETE SOLDIERS OF BENGHAZI, WHY RELIGOUS REFORMS MUST BE PUTO NT HE TABLE

I'm not going to discussion the 9/11 attacks on Benghazi, Libya. If you wish to watch the film then please do so. Like "Black Hawk Down" it irritates me to see a constructive "Humanitarian Intervention" policy turned into a "Boots on the Ground" military policy...

What I wish to talk about is the need for "Religious Reforms" to be placed on the table for discussion. Much of the 9/11 attacks on the United States, and in Benghazi was from radicalized Muslims, many of which were armed against Gadhafi by American State Department and CIA, or at least that was the impression I got from talking with Diplomats/Sr. Advisors that were traveling with Ambassador Stevens and the film "`2 Hours-The Secrete Soldiers of Benghazi", this was obviously counterproductive and got Americans killed *as I had warned the Sr. Advisor, whom deleted me from his Facebook after heated discussions…*

We must bridge the gap between faiths and come to common interest of people wishing to put a roof over their head, feed their family, educate them and establish a quality of life…

Christians must reach out and realize that Jesus was one of the 1st Religious Reformers. He started by kicking the money changers out of the Temple." We need to kick the moneychangers out of political policy making that is squandering trillions of dollars and American blood... I've said it before and I will say it again "America's common Defense has lost its commonsense."

America was spending nearly 1/2 Trillion a year in the Middle East and Africa and there is less Peace and security as a result....

*For far too long the belief in God has been exploited, and God`s name invoked for* the evil deeds of man, and profits "Christianity and other religions have all been manipulated throughout history by barbaric, insulting and criminality towards humanity "One of the worst perversions of Religion is the radicalization of Islam." It is so sad that the Sharia Law` is interpreted so radically and contrary to humanity."

The Law`s practitioners quickly point to the outside as opposed to taking a good look in the mirror and into their own hearts and minds to avoid realizing that their thoughts and deeds are perverse, ugly, ignorant, and damaging to mankind and that the radical practices have no place in the World.

So many of the great leaders in the world such as Jesus, Buddha, and other mystical beings that God graced the World with during our short span of human history ALL: practiced a benevolent, understanding, and profound love and equality for humanity. "

Yet, historical power seekers have interpreted these wonderments in such *horrific ways that they deserve humanities admonishments. Christianity, with all its horrible warfare, crusades, turning a blind eye on the Holocaust, subjugation of women (Today as well as in the past), and patriarchal excesses have issues as well. All Religions have had a less than pious past." I have no doubts that Jesus, or God would-not approve "of their actions."*

Islamic practice has also has a long history of horrible, despicable and violent behaviors that sadly has become pretty much an accepted practice by today`s mainstream Islamic society. That same society under Sharia Law oppresses the individual into forced submission, and only offers death as the alternative " If that is not bad enough, the world is not even allowed to gaze upon a beautiful God given smile of an Islamic girl or woman.

Extreme Islam accepts the disfiguring of those young and beautiful faces by condoning the "Evil" throwing of Acid into their faces." Moreover, society debates whether or not water-boarding is bad."

Religious Reforms must come from within. Be it from within Christianity, Hinduism, Judaism and most certainly Islam.

There must be an internal rise and admonish of these religious faults." Like Jesus throwing the moneychangers from the Temple all Religions must also kick the moneychangers and the power hungry manipulators of the masses out of God`s Temples."

I see that there is an undoubtedly strong case for Religious Reforms" For far too long the Individual "that follows these religions have been silent and co-conspired by doing nothing." It is not the Muslims to point to the Catholics for abusing children, when they have their own practices of abuse. It is not the Christians to point towards the Muslims for their faults, or the Jews to point to fingers for not accepting any intermediary to God."

It is every individual's responsibility to question these religions that participate in them and to let them know that they are freaking crazy practices that are causing vast hardships, oppression, death and destruction upon humanity." It is the individual practitioner to call for change in these perversions of God's gift of life."

Thank you, and truly God Bless all of you to be given the strength to rise up and kick these money changers, and profiteers out of the Temples of the World, and our Governments...

10
RUSSIAN VETO
IN THE
UNITED NATIONS SECURITY
COUNCIL END IN SUPPORT OF
ASSAD OF SYRIA, AND
YANUKOVYCH MASS MURDERS

The United Nations has lost its focus on the "United Nations Declaration of Human Rights" and constructive policy making. It is becoming more of a "Grandstanding" podium than a place to solve problems...

The United Nations must work, or the world will see far worse problems than that occurring in Syria...

We see this with Russia's Putin and Medvedev's sided with Assad of Syria, as they did with the Yanukovych regime in Ukraine. Both positions are quite crazy as both the Syrian and Ukrainian regimes slaughtered "Peacefully Protesters" to try to maintain personal power...

In both Syria and Ukraine, I and a vast majority of the world favored "Peaceful Protest," and the hope of peaceful outcomes...

I as a Global Citizen wrote many position papers calling for power-sharing and/or the call for snap elections to prevent violence.

I also wrote and personally asked the U.S. Defense Attaché to work close with the Ukrainian Minister of Defense to ensure that the Army was not sent into the streets of Kiev. I knew if the Army was sent in that Yanukovych like al Assad would have no problem slaughtering peaceful protesters.

In Kiev, it could have resulted in 10's of thousands of Peaceful Protesters being killed... Fortunately, only Yanukovych Snipers were sent in that cost the lives of about 100 "The Heavenly Hundred"... The Ukrainian Minister of Defense had listened to the American Defense Attaché', refused orders to send in the Army...

I strongly feel this decision saved 10's of thousands if not hundreds of thousands of people. For sure the Revolution would have started in Kiev a City of 4 million that would have torn apart...

I will not spend a great deal of time on Ukraine; however, I will mention that I am writing a book on Ukraine. The following photo is the draft cover. I will mention that both Ukraine and Syria's Heads of State failed to look at constructive leadership options. Both chose Mass Murder as their way of trying to hold onto power instead of simply working to serving the people. Granted Yanukovych was elected to serve, while al Assad was a Dictator that was self-serving, but both were quite similar... Both were self-serving.

"THE UNELECTED PRESIDENT"

UKRAINE

"Return to Revolution"
By
Harvey Carroll,
Jr.

At the end of the Ukrainian Revolution the Ukraine's President Yanukovych sent in Water Cannons and Snipers that killed the "Heavenly Hundred" and Syria slaughtered protesters and began bombing cities...

Both countries have ended up in conflict as a result of such brutal treatment of civilians, with Syria far more devastating at this time. Yet, if Russia continues on a destructive policy making path, it could lead to mass death and destruction in Ukraine... I know the mindset ant it is primed for such destruction, with few focusing on decentralization and reforms, or real plans to do either...

Fortunately, spending a great deal in Ukraine, I have managed to write position papers to continue the Democratic and peace promotion process. (Note, I was shocked that a Revolution occurred, and there was little Parliamentary actions that could have been taken to prevent mass corruption, and/or constructive trade negotiations.

Once the protest began those that I knew that were involved had a very difficult time. They were beaten, killed and in constant fear... I talked with some of them, and they wanted to arm themselves. While I understood their situation, I encouraged them to remain peaceful... I tried to remind them of great men like Ghandi, and Martin Luther King that led constructive peaceful "non-violent" protest and gained World support…

I also reminded them that they would all most likely be killed if they tried to arm themselves.   The corrupt Yanukovych Administration was looking for any excuse to send in troops. If arms were found in the streets, he would certainly use it as an excuse to send in the Army…

I wrote and even called them many times encouraging them to stay peaceful, despite their continued complaints that they were being attacked and often beaten).

After the Revolution I tried to prevent Civil Conflict and advised caution on any Anti-Terror Operations to deal with the Russian backed Separatist in the East of Ukraine. The Separatist in the East began taking City and other Government Buildings by Armed Force...

I strongly believed that sharing the same thoughts that brought about the Revolution could be the solution to gain support of the people in Donetsk and Luhansk. Yet, this opportunity failed as Russia began to back the Separatists.

The new Ukrainian Government was failing in their offering of Decentralization of Political and Economic Reforms... The buzz word of "Reform, Reform, Reform, and Decentralization, Decentralization, Decentralization" became the talk of the region, but few knew how to do it…

I knew very well that it would take "Comprehensive Planning" and well educated and organized Professional Public Administrators, but there were few, if any ready to take on such task to be between Politicians "Bullshit Artist" Business that represents special interest, and Citizens Social Wants that think the Government should do everything…

I talked with and even shared a 25 page "Comprehensive Plan" that could go a long way in these efforts to decentralize; however, the Economic Development and Trade Minister was replaced by someone less focused and in my opinion far less understanding of such policies.

Yet, the Separatist began taking the Airport in Donetsk – scrapping and looting the ½ billion dollar economic hub of the region... The new Ukrainian Government sent in the Army to try to secure the airport that turned into a long-term back and forth fight that latterly scrapped the ½ billion dollar airport along with the economic hub of Donetsk Region...

In addition to experienced "De-escalation and Decentralization" concepts, the sharing of well written "Comprehensive Planning" templates that presented an easy to follow step by step for Decentralization Reforms was never promoted. Such plans could have offered a clear road map for Public-Private-Partnerships, Civil Society Participation with Government... Such Comprehensive Planning is key to any

Professional Public Administration and real Reforms...

I went further by offering negotiation frameworks to key Ukrainian negotiators prior to and during the Minsk I and II Agreement process. I even offered possible solutions for Minsk III via a "Crimean Compromise"...

The "Crimean Compromise" would have a key focus on backing the fighting forces back; thereby, creating a "Green zone" to allowing OSCE Inspectors to monitor and reduce conflict in Ukraine...

NOTE: (Similar situations will ultimately be needed in Syria, as will a "Divide Syria" and perhaps even parts of Iraq via "Pizza Politics," but this is going to take Men or Women of great resolve that focus on peace and not so much profiteering)...

I encouraged the UN to ask Assad to step down and call for elections... At that time; before the violence, I really felt that

Assad could step down and win the Presidency in Syria, and open up a constructive Democracy... But his demonic dictatorship mentality prevented reason and rational thinking that served his citizens best interest...

Gadhafi could have also in Libya; however, the Dictator mind is that of force instead of governmental foundations that give people a voice... Yanukovych had even less difficulties to deal with, he simply had to look at Trade and Economic reforms... But, all three Gadhafi, Assad and Yanukovych chose Mass Murder as opposed to constructive leadership and/or simple professional public administration...

The "Dictator Mindset" was clear with Gadhafi and Assad and it was evident that they were never going to step down. Nor would either ever call for elections to give people a voice, but the United Nations should have tried harder...

Perhaps snap elections could have resulted in preventing civil conflict, and by stepping down opened up the possibility of being elected to power. We have seen successful Politicians stay in power for decades because they listened to their constituent's voices and/or made their constituents believe they were listening...

11
CONCLUSIONS

Failures at the United Nations "Humanitarian Intervention" allowed grandstanding that led to Russia supporting Mass Murders in both Syria and Ukraine... This is an obvious failure of not only the United Nations, but also Personal, and failures for Humanity...

The United Nations must-try to change this mindset--neither Putin/Medvedev, nor "any" United Nations member should be allowed to support Mass Murder.

The World clearly sees where it leads. Russia's support Mass Murders in both Syria and in Ukraine, and ignored Gadhafi's massacre to justify Russia's' UN Security Councils VETO against Syrian Humanitarian Intervention.

If a clearer case for Humanity been presented, and Russia had been a more constructive United Nations partners focusing on Diplomacy and constructive solutions in Syria we would not see Civil Conflict, the vast death, fleeing and rise of terrorism we see today...

The Russian United Nations Security Council VETO against Syrian Humanitarian Intervention led to major civil conflict in Syria that cost more than 300,000 lives, and over 4 million refugees fleeing the war zone cold homeless and hungry, as well as a vast increase in Terrorism that we are now seeing in the Middle East, France, and from Africa, to include the recent downing of passenger jet full of Russian civilians...

So I ask the world and Russia "Was my Intervention so bad in Libya?" Absolutely, it100% it was constructive, with a few flaws; however, it is far from the failures that were created in Syrian policy, and the United Nations and certainly Russia should be assumed for creating such death and destruction...

"Libya"

**My suggestion for the United Nations
"Humanitarian Intervention"
(THE UNELECTED PRESIDENT)
By
Harvey Carroll, Jr.**

I'm a former U.S. Army Military Policeman/Investigator, turned high level political junkie. I made the suggestion for "Humanitarian Intervention" into Libya; however, I favored a "Divide Libya" policy that would have prevented Civil Conflict, the death of Gadhafi and a Libyan failed state...

I now hold a Bachelors of Business Administration Degree specializing in Real Estate and Finance, and three partial Masters in Business, Public Administration as well as Diplomacy and International Commerce...

I've been considered the most influential international political figure in Kentucky-US, and some would say that perhaps in the World at one time. I have dealt with Governors, Senators, Presidents and Foreign Heads of State; and in the process I have saved millions of lives, and affected the economic fate of nations... Yet, I have made mistakes, and even cost lives and often ponder if the "End Justified the Means."

It has always been quite easy for me to deal with complex U.S. National and International Policy. From a young age I dealt with local, state, national and international policy that includes Latin America i.e. "Panama," Middle East (Iraq, Libya, Syria, Israel, Iran), Africa, and even coming to the AID after the collapse of the Soviet Union to protect U.S. and Global Security by suggesting buying out the nuclear weapons to prevent them from ending up on the Black Market for Terrorism, as well as preventing the former fifteen Soviet States against each other.

I also suggested financial bailouts, and another financial AID **via** the IFC/World Bank for Ukraine that saved seventy-five banks a few years ago (a similar plan presented to the U.S. House and Senate Financial Services Committee "Frank and Dodd" to bailout the American Economy to assist 2/3rds of the American States and Top Banks from Collapse.

More recently, I have shared suggestions to have the OSCE get between the separatist and the Ukrainian Army to the Ukrainian Presidents people tasked to negotiate the Minsk Agreements that may have prevented Ukraine from turning into another Syria... In the process I have noticed that Russian President Putin sent Troops "Little Green Men" into Crimea; thereby, I responded by sharing "Peace Negotiations" and a "Crimean Compromise"...

www.ingramcontent.com/pod-product-compliance
Lightning Source LLC
Chambersburg PA
CBHW071246280526
45788CB00004B/1601